TOO CUTE! BABY ANIMALS

Baby Bears

by Colleen Sexton

Kaleidoscope
Minneapolis, MN

Where the Quest for Discovery Begins

This edition first published in 2024 by Kaleidoscope Publishing, Inc.

Kaleidoscope Publishing, Inc.
6012 Blue Circle Drive
Minnetonka, MN 55343

Library of Congress Control Number
2023936784

ISBN
978-1-64519-697-6 (library bound)
978-1-64519-745-4 (ebook)

Bigfoot Jr. lurks within one of the images in this book. It's up to you to find him!

Table of Contents

Hello, Cubs!

A cold winter wind blows outside. But a mother bear is warm in her **den**. There, she gives birth to a **litter** of tiny babies. They are called cubs.

Bears make dens in hollow logs, under rocks, or in caves. They might dig tunnels underground or in the snow.

The cubs drink creamy milk
from their mother's body.
It helps them grow fast.

The mother bear does not eat during her winter sleep. She lives off her body fat.

The cubs curl up next to their mother. She keeps them safe and warm as they sleep.

FUN FACT

Bear cubs cannot see when they are born. Their eyes open when they are about one month old.

From Nose to Toes

Spring is here! The cubs follow their mother out of the den.

A furry cub **stretches** its rounded body. The cub has a small tail and a large head.

Bear cubs have thick fur that keeps them warm and dry. Different kinds of bears have different colored fur.

brown bear

polar bear

black bear

giant panda

The cub walks on four short legs. Its wide, padded paws leave tracks.

FUN FACT

Most mammals walk on their toes. Bears walk on flat feet like people.

Each paw has five toes. Each toe has a long **claw**. Claws help the cub dig and climb.

The cub looks around with its small eyes. It listens with its furry, round ears.

The cub sniffs the air with its large nose. There are so many new smells!

Bears can pick up a smell that is one mile (1.6 kilometers) or more away. Their sense of smell is one of the strongest in the world!

FUN FACT

Sometimes a bear stands on its back legs to get a better view.

Parts of a Cub

Bear Facts

Kind of Animal: mammal

Size at Birth: from the size of a stick of butter to the size of a loaf of bread

Litter Size: one to five cubs

Home: mostly in forests, mountains, grasslands, and sea ice in North America, Asia, and Europe

Traveling Together

The mother bear and her cubs set off in search of food.

Sometimes a cub gets a ride on its mother's back!

The cubs climb trees to find fruit and nuts. They learn to fish. They dig for roots and bugs.

FUN FACT

Many bears like sweet treats. A bear will tear apart a beehive to get to the honey inside.

A mother bear looks out for **predators**. She fights off any animal that tries to take her cubs.

The cubs stop to play. They chase each other. *ROWR!* They growl as they pretend to fight.

The cubs rest. Sometimes they pile on their mother to nap.

The mother and cubs keep moving. They eat as much as they can. They need to put on weight for the winter.

FUN FACT

A bear cub stays with its mother for up to three years. Then it lives on its own.

The weather gets colder. The mother and cubs make a new den. They are ready for another long sleep.

Photo Glossary

claws: a sharp, curved nail at the end of an animal's toe

den: a place where an animal lives and gives birth

litter: a group of babies born at one time; most mother bears have two cubs in each litter.

mammals: warm-blooded animals that have hair or fur; mammals drink their mother's milk.

predators: animals that hunt and eat other animals; tigers, wolves, bobcats, and coyotes are some predators that are a danger to bear cubs.

stretches: reaches the arms, legs, or whole body their full length

Read More

Marie, Renata. *Black Bears.* Minneapolis, Minn.: Kaleidoscope Books, 2021.

Myers, Maya. *Little Kids First Big Book of Baby Animals.* Washington, D.C.: National Geographic Kids, 2022.

Szymanski, Jennifer. *All About Bears.* Washington, D.C.: National Geographic Kids, 2019.

Websites

FACTSURFER

Factsurfer.com gives you a safe, fun way to find more information.

1. Go to www.factsurfer.com.
2. Enter "Baby Bears" into the search box and click 🔍
3. Select your book cover to see a list of related websites.

About the Author

Colleen Sexton is a writer and editor. She is the author of more than 100 nonfiction books for kids on topics ranging from astronauts to glaciers to elephants. She lives in Minnesota.

INDEX

PHOTO CREDITS

The images in this book are reproduced through the courtesy of: Nataliia Melnychuk/Shutterstock Images, cover; Volodymyr Burdiak/Shutterstock Images, title page, 15; Jeff McGraw/Shutterstock Images, p. 3; Rosa Jay/Shutterstock Images, p. 4, 23; Volodymyr Burdiak/Shutterstock Images, p. 4–5 (top); Lars Ove Jonsson/Shutterstock Images, p. 4–5 (bottom); Erik Mandre/Shutterstock Images, p. 6 (top); MM.Wildlifephotos/Shutterstock Images, p. 6 (bottom); Volodymyr Burdiak/Shutterstock Images, p. 7; WildMedia/Shutterstock Images, p. 8; Eric Isselee/Shutterstock Images, p. 9 (polar bear); Volodymyr Burdiak/Shutterstock Images, p. 9 (brown bear); Wonderly Imaging/Shutterstock Images, p. 9 (giant panda); Holly Kuchera/Shutterstock Images, p. 9 (black bear); David Rasmus/Shutterstock Images, p. 10 (top); Sergey Uryadnikov/Shutterstock Images, p. 10 (bottom); Jo Crebbin/Shutterstock Images, p. 11; Geoffrey Kuchera/Shutterstock Images, p. 12; Volodymyr Burdiak/Shutterstock Images, p. 13; Rosa Jay/Shutterstock Images, p. 14; Richard Seeley/Shutterstock Images, p. 16 (top); Malyshev1974/Shutterstock Images, p. 16 (bottom); DONOT6_STUDIO/Shutterstock Images, p. 17 (honeycomb); Alexander Piragis/Shutterstock Images, p. 17; Scott E Read/Shutterstock Images, p. 18 (top); GUDKOV ANDREY/Shutterstock Images, p. 18 (bottom); David Rasmus/Shutterstock Images, p. 19; Tony Campbell/Shutterstock Images, p. 20–21; Volodymyr Burdiak/Shutterstock Images, p. 21; Jo Crebbin/Shutterstock Images, p. 22 (claws); Lars Ove Jonsson/Shutterstock Images, p. 22 (den); Volodymyr Burdiak/Shutterstock Images, p. 22 (litter); Erik Mandre/Shutterstock Images, p. 22 (mammals); Ana Gram/Shutterstock Images, p. 22 (predators); Volodymyr Burdiak/Shutterstock Images, p. 22 (stretches).